Raccoon Rescue

KAMA EINHORN
PHOTOGRAPHS BY SHELLY ROSS

HOUGHTON MIFFLIN HARCOURT
Boston   New York

Library of Congress Cataloging-in-Publication Data is available.
ISBN 978-1-328-76705-9

Manufactured in Malaysia
TWP 10 9 8 7 6 5 4 3 2 1
4500745382

This book is based on the true stories of rescued raccoons, and it's full of real facts about these wild animals. But it's also "creative" nonfiction—because raccoons don't talk, at least not in ways that humans can understand! Some raccoons in this story are combinations of several different ones, and certain details, including locations, events, and timing have been changed, and some human dialogue has been reconstructed from memory.

This book is not a manual on how to rescue wildlife, or provide any actual directions on caring for raccoons or any other species. Every situation and every animal are different. If you see an animal in trouble, contact a licensed wildlife rehabilitator right away.

For Shelly Ross and the entire WildCare team of San Rafael,

California, and for all the vulnerable wildlife in Marin County

—K. E.

For WildCare, which allows me this incredible opportunity.

And for Christine and Kim, without whom I wouldn't have

survived my first season.

—S. R.

CONTENTS

HOPE & HAVEN:
ANIMAL SANCTUARIES

A sanctuary is a place where living beings are kept safe from harm and are free to be themselves.

Humans have created animal sanctuaries—protected places for injured, orphaned, or threatened animals. In sanctuaries, people prepare animals for their return to the wild. If that's not an option, the animals spend the rest of their lives being protected in as natural a habitat as possible.

At WildCare in San Rafael, California, the staff (and about four hundred volunteers) helps nearly four thousand animals every year—urban wildlife creatures such as raccoons, birds, skunks, opossums, and squirrels.

At animal sanctuaries, humans lend a helping hand.

Welcome to WildCare!

Animal sanctuaries exist for different reasons, but 90 percent of the animals at WildCare are there because of human interference. People have built houses or buildings that force animals out of their homes. They've put roads through animals' territories, so wildlife is more likely to be hit by cars. Some people consider particular animals to be pests. (Raccoons get into people's garbage and sometimes even into their homes and make messes, so people have them exterminated.)

Over the past two hundred years, more than half of the raccoon ranges in the United States and Canada have increased in area, as the animals have learned to live in cities and suburbs, near humans. But the ranges of their larger predators (cougars, bobcats, coyotes, wolves) have gotten smaller. There are more raccoons than ever before because there are fewer big predators (they're losing their habitats, too, and being trapped and killed by humans). Raccoons have the same problems, of course, but

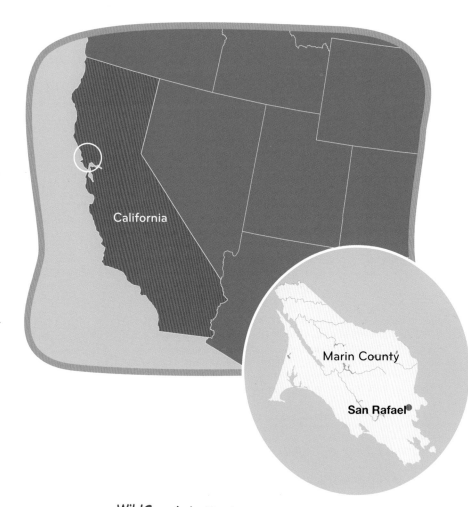

California

Marin County

San Rafael

WildCare is in Marin County, California,
in the small city of San Rafael.

they're really good at adapting to challenges.

The people who run sanctuaries are serious about their work, but they wish they didn't have to do this work in the first place. They wish there was no more need for animal sanctuaries and that the world was safer for animals. They teach their communities about how to exist peacefully with wildlife and how to share their habitats.

There can be plenty of heartbreak in any sanctuary's story, but there are also lots of happy endings. Also, the more you know about why sanctuaries are important and what people can do to help, the better off all animals—in your neighborhood and across the globe—will be.

SANCTUARY STEPS

Each sanctuary is different, but they all do some or all of the following things, in the order below. WildCare handles all four phases:

- **Rescue:** Humans step in, remove animals from harm, and bring them to safety. Rescue situations are usually emergencies.

- **Recovery:** Licensed wildlife caregivers treat the animals for injuries or illnesses, create a recovery plan, and let them rest and heal. With raccoon babies, this stage gives them the space, time, food, and support they need until they're big enough to live safely in the wild.

- **Rehabilitation:** The caregivers encourage the animals' natural instincts so they can return to the wild. Some "wild" behaviors have to be taught, and some the animals simply know. Sometimes, the animals must learn by watching one another.

- **Release:** Using a careful process, caregivers help animals return to their natural habitats and live in the way they were meant to.

A MARVELOUS, MOSSY WORLD

These woods are wide and wet and wild. These woods are soft and green and mossy. And now these woods are our new home.

We knew exactly what to do when we got here, even though we're only twenty weeks old. Here we are, living where we were supposed to live all along. We've been out here for four whole days and nights, and believe us . . . this is where we're gonna stay!

Since we were two weeks old, we've been cooped up inside a house with this one human, named Shelly. Then we lived in a big cage outside, built just for raccoons like us, to get us ready for the real woods. A whole team of people took care of us along the way.

The four of us are a team, too. No matter what, we've stuck together.

It's October, and since we got out here, we've been super-busy exploring and finding food, but things will really slow down when we find our dens in November. We'll sleep more and eat and drink less, all through the winter.

Here we are...
The Fab Four
in the forest!

Once we make it through this first winter, we'll be "wilded up" for sure. The human world will be far behind us. Who knows? We may have forgotten what books look like, even though we grew up in an apartment full of bookshelves.

So we're going to remember it all before we forget . . . with this memory book.

I'm Mr. Green, and me and my three littermates will tell our happy and sad story here.

PART 1

RESCUE

Human Hands

CHAPTER 1

AS HELPLESS AS LEMONS

Like most raccoons in Northern California, we were born in May. At two weeks old, all four of us were the size of lemons.

We were about as helpless as lemons, too. Our eyes and ears still hadn't opened. All we knew was our mom's warm milk and the feeling of one another's heartbeats. I bet you could almost see our hearts thumping through our pink skin. We had the tiniest bit of light silver fuzz, with none at all on our bellies (you could even see our belly buttons!). We didn't look anything like the big kids we've grown into. We weren't clever, naughty, or ready for challenges . . . yet.

We were clueless, but we were fine. We were safe in a nest in an attic, right where the ceiling came to a point. Just before we were born, our mom tore out the itchy insulation to make a nice safe nest (raccoons can squeeze and scramble into small places). She gave birth right there, and there we stayed. It was tight and cozy, like a tree nook. Raccoons are never far from trees!

Our nest was the only place we knew, but millions of raccoons live all over the United States (except Alaska and Hawaii) and in parts of Canada and Mexico. Most of us live in habitats where there is plenty of water (forests, swamps, and marshes), but there are plenty of us in cities and suburbs, where we can scavenge for food. In Toronto, Ontario, there are as many raccoons as there are people!

Anyway, our mom had made a hole in the attic wall to get in and out. We raccoons are experts at finding places to live (such as our attic or crawlspaces under houses) when our natural habitat is destroyed because people have built houses, buildings, or roads. Many of us make our nests in chimneys because they feel like hollow trees.

Lots of times we outsmart the humans. Some of them don't like that at all.

Anyway, on our two-week birthday, we knew something was very wrong. Our mom had gone out for food and hadn't come back in three whole days. Female raccoons are very good moms; they don't just abandon their kits (that's what you call raccoon babies). If they have to move us to a new den, they count us to make sure we're all there, and they come back an extra time to be sure they haven't left any of us behind. We rely on our moms for a long time. When everything goes right, we nurse for twelve weeks, then stay with our moms for almost a year. We even den with her over our first winter. But things didn't go right for us.

We huddled for warmth in our little fluff pile, but we got hungrier and thirstier. We were so cold, we were almost numb. We already felt like a team, four hearts thumping in one small heap, but in our tiny hearts we knew there was a big problem. Our mom must have been trapped—or worse—out there.

Lots of people think that raccoons are a big nuisance. We get into garbage cans and make a huge mess. We'll eat any kind of leftovers—pizza crusts, potato chips, bits of meat left on a chicken bone, you name it! That's what makes us omnivores and scavengers. Hey, when our natural habitat shrinks, we have to get food somewhere, and as we've lost more of our habitat, we've gotten even better at finding food. And we don't know how to clean up (or why that's so important to humans)!

The family who lived in the house hadn't known there was a nest in the attic until they heard us crying: *eep, eep, eep*. These people, like most humans, didn't want to hurt us, but humans don't always know what to do when there are raccoons living in their attic. I guess they figured it out, because they called a wildlife rescue group and clinic called WildCare. The staff told them that someone was on the way.

Gloved human hands pulled us out of our nest one at a time, wrapping us in a soft cloth. We wiggled and wriggled, squealed and squirmed, and pawed and scratched at the air with our claws. But the human hands were gentle, and we settled down and let them touch us. And anyway, we really had no choice.

They held our cold bodies in their giant hands.

We were young, but we knew the truth. If humans can touch a wild animal of any age or size, something has gone terribly wrong.

One by one, they set each of us carefully into a cardboard box that had air holes. We'd been high up in the attic, just as other litters are high up in trees. But suddenly we were low . . . on the ground . . . in the human world.

We were still together in our cozy pile, but our life would never be the same. The top of the box closed. Now the humans were in charge.

CHAPTER 2

THE KINDNESS OF STRANGERS

The humans drove us a few miles to WildCare in the small city of San Rafael and rushed us into the exam room. The head of their raccoon team, Marie-Noelle, was waiting. The vibe smelled serious. The vet, Dr. Juliana, and the clinic manager, Melanie, pulled us out of the box one by one. They stayed calm and took their time, so we did too, even though the clinic was really busy. Lots of animals—skunks, squirrels, birds, opossums, and more—are born in spring. It was like an emergency room.

Dr. Juliana and Marie-Noelle knew right away that we had hypothermia—we were way too cold. Our bodies couldn't control

We fit right into their palms, and a bright light warmed our skin.

26

our temperatures the way they would when we got bigger. We had been depending on our mom to do that, but the human team knew how to do it, too. They microwaved towels until they were nice and warm, but not too hot, and wrapped us up as if we were miniature burritos! When those towels started to cool, the team had more warm ones waiting. Everyone moved quietly.

They set us gently on a tiny scale and recorded our weights.

Just by looking at our tummies, the people could tell that we were starving. But before they could give us any milk, they had to rehydrate us. Our bodies just didn't have enough water in them. We wouldn't have been able to digest any food (we could have gotten diarrhea, which can kill us!). So they

Their hands knew exactly how to touch us.

heated up some special liquid that human babies also get when they're dehydrated. They pulled apart our lips and used a small syringe to push in some liquid. They also gave us water under our skin with a needle, so our bodies would absorb it (this didn't hurt at all). They kept doing all this until we peed!

They found fleas on all of us, which let them know that our mom had been missing for at least a few days. They combed them out with teeny, tiny combs. They also rubbed our bottoms with cloth to make us pee and poop, which our mom would have done until we were old enough to do it on our own.

They used stethoscopes to listen to our lungs, which sounded "crackly." This meant that we might have respiratory infections, so we all got antibiotics. Then the humans ran their hands over our bodies to feel for fractures.

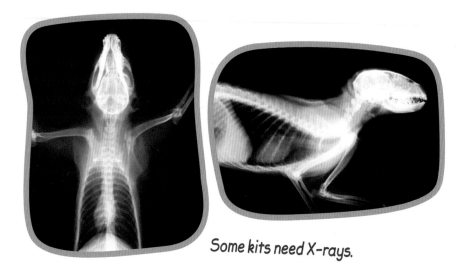

Some kits need X-rays.

We were super-weak, so they had to look carefully to see that our legs were held in the right position, not twisted or draggy.

Once they'd finished examining us, they moved us to an incubator in Ward C, a small room with a STAFF ONLY sign on the door. (When we came back for our checkups, there were a baby skunk, a baby coyote, and a litter of squirrels in Ward C!)

GREEN

Patient # ...SLO... Admit Date ...4/30... Band/Microchip # ......
985 112 006 577 821   Scanned ☐

Species .... Raccoon .... Sex: M / O / U   Age: A / J / F / N

story .... Mom left in a hurry

RED
Meds

WildCare Intake Exam

Time .... 12 ... am / pm   Meds ...D₅₀ ... mm

Examiner .... NS

Weight .... 46.4 ... g / kg / lb

Fluids .... 12u cc ... sq / iv / po

Temp ....

Vocal, warm, active, NAI

4u Electrostat

~~cold electrostat~~

8cc electrostat mix ⎫
18cc sq us   ⎬ 3pm

8cc electrostat/T. Factor mix @ 5pm
~~4cc electrostat~~

Initial Treatment Plan ... Raccoon Treatment Plan
Age at Intake 5 days   DOB: 4/25/16
Weaning (7-9 wks) 6/13 - 6/27
(begin 7 end 9 wks)
FVRCP 3x Q14D 6/13, 6/27, 7/11
(7, 9, 11 wks)
CDAP 3x Q14D 6/13, 6/27, 7/11
(7, 9, 11 wks)
To Runs (12 wks) 7/18
Release (17-22 wks) 8/22 - 9/26

☐ INCUBATOR   ☐ HEATING PAD   ☐ TO FOSTER CARE Age Estimate: ......

YELLOW
Follow Up

Body Condition

plump   good   okay
thin   emaciated

Weight Range ......

Dehydration
☐ Not Dehydrated
☐ MILD < 7%
☐ MODERATE < 9%
☐ SEVERE 10%+

Initial Bloodwork Date
PCV Intake ......
BC Intake ......
TP Intake ......

Initial Fecal Date ......

Wet Mount Date ......

Wormer/Vaccine Record

Date	Dose/Drug
5/27	Strongid
6/13	FVRCPV #1
6/13	CDAP #1
6/13	Strongid
6/27	Strongid .3
6/27	FVRCPV #2
6/27	CDAP #2
7/17	FVRCPV #3
7/17	CDAP #3
7/17	Strongid
7/31	Strongid

DISPOSITION Date 9/7
Location (st., city) ... Fairfax

☐ AWOL   ☐ DOA   ☐ DON
☐ EXP   ☐ EXP 24 hrs.   ☐ EU
☐ EU 24 hrs.   ☐ TRANS   ☑ REL
☐ CONSULT   ☐ REUNITE

DB Entry: ......   LB Entry: SR

DIAGNOSTICS   Close-out form complete? ☐ Y ☐ N
Lab Work Sent: PID# ......
Type ......   Date ......
Findings/Results/Necropsy Notes: ......

Date ......   Initials ......

They started a record for each of us.

31

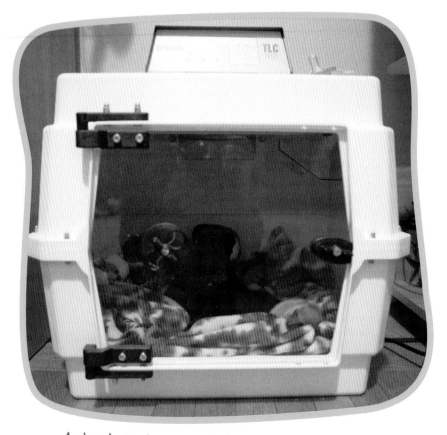

An incubator is a warm box. Look closely for the kit.

Every animal that comes through this clinic
has a different story. Some of us come as
litters, some alone. Some of us are tiny, some
adults. Most raccoons come because our
moms were trapped and moved far from

their litters, or even killed. Aside from our situation, there are two other main reasons why WildCare has to step in:

- Den problems. This is when dens have been messed up or destroyed by people cutting down trees or doing construction or repairs on sheds, garages, decks, roofs, chimneys, or attics. Or, if there's a heat wave, our den might get too hot, and we might try to leave and then get into trouble. Or a predator (such as a bobcat or coyote) can attack a mom and her kits in a nest, and those that survive the attack can't live on their own.

- Separated from mom. When our eyes are still closed and mom is using her mouth to move us by the scruffs of our necks from one place to another, we can fall and be left behind. Even when we're older, we can become separated if we are chased by a dog, or we can get into something we can't get out of, such as a dumpster.

But no matter what had happened to any of us, these humans were ready to help.

This four-week-old litter came in the same day as we did.

CHAPTER 3
GOLDEN HILLS

Marie-Noelle called Shelly, a volunteer foster caregiver in San Francisco, right away. Shelly had been waiting for this call. She usually gets "assigned" to her litter in the very beginning of May, but now it was the middle. Shelly was about to drive up to WildCare for her weekly volunteer shift, when she cleans cages and does whatever needs to be done, which is usually a lot.

"Come on up, Shelly, but you can forget about your shift tonight," Marie-Noelle said. "You'll be turning right around and heading home. Your litter's here. Four two-week-olds, found alone in an attic. Dehydrated and starving and full of fleas. But they're in pretty good shape now. They're stable, hydrated, and ready for you."

"I'm on my way," Shelly said. "And you know me. I'm sorry they're in this situation, but I'm so ready to help!" She'd already taken her supplies out of the closet, organized them, and set them out, just waiting for us. She's used them every spring for five years (one year she had twenty-seven raccoon babies, spread out over four or five months!), and next year she'll use them again. Our lives totally fill her home!

We were lifted from the incubator. They wrapped each of us snugly in cloth, heads and all, like miniature burritos, and put us back in the box, which was full of warm fleece. Now it had some portable heating pads inside! Soon we were back in a car, moving fast over the Golden Gate Bridge, up and down steep hills, until we got to Shelly's apartment in San Francisco.

Kit Supplies

- ☑ incubator
- ☑ bottles
- ☑ syringes
- ☑ needles
- ☑ heating pad
- ☑ formula
- ☑ thermometer
- ☑ flannel and fleece blankets and sheets
- ☑ hard cat carrier
- ☑ pet wee-wee pads
- ☑ cotton swabs, cotton balls
- ☑ tissues
- ☑ scale
- ☑ feeding and weight charts
- ☑ clipboard
- ☑ pacifiers
- ☑ playpen
- ☑ litter-box
- ☑ cans of wet puppy food
- ☑ bags of dry puppy food
- ☑ cat beds
- ☑ carpeted climbing tree
- ☑ cabinet stocked with all medicine
- ☑ about 50 different toys

During that whole ride, Shelly let us know
important things. Our ears weren't open yet,
and she wasn't even talking out loud, but we
could feel her vibe. "I got-choo," she was
telling us. "You guys are going to be okay. I
know how to take care of you, and you've got
one another, too." Still, we huddled together
as close as we could.

Now we were on the twisting, turning road
to becoming big, healthy raccoons. Just
like on the hills of this city, there were ups
and downs on this road too. But we made it
through months with a human, and now here
we are.

Here's how we've grown since that day.

GROWING UP RACCOON

We start life as tiny as kiwis!

By two weeks, we're the size of lemons or avocados.

39

By four weeks,
we're the size of
small eggplants.

By six weeks...
bigger eggplants.

40

At eight weeks, we're the size of a butternut squash.

And by ten weeks, we're like footballs that have legs and tails.

41

By the time we're released, we're at least eight pounds—about the size of a newborn human. And we're still growing! We'll grow up to thirteen pounds, but some males may grow up to twenty-three pounds.

RECOVERY

Kit Care

CHAPTER 4

GETTING to KNOW US

Shelly carried our box into her apartment and set it on the floor of a small, empty room that was reserved just for us. It was quiet and warm. There were no drafts, and sunlight poured in all day long. She moved us into a plastic cat carrier that had lots of fleece at the bottom, and she set that inside a playpen (one made for human babies!). Then she covered our carrier with a towel. It was our new nest, and it felt good.

Our bodies stayed at the right temperature, thanks to some stuffed animals filled with heated gel packs. But we could wiggle away from them if we got too hot.

The kits in raccoon litters are almost impossible to tell apart, and we don't get names the way pets do, because we're not pets. Still, Shelly had to tell us apart so that each of us could get the right bottle with the right amount of formula (different amounts depending on our weights). And she had to know which kit was supposed to get which medicine. And she had to tell us apart when she weighed us every day.

Shelly kept careful charts so that she and the staff at WildCare could make sure we were growing normally.

At the clinic, Marie-Noelle had brushed each of us with a tiny bit of whiteout in different places (one of us got a white smudge on our right ear, one on the left ear, one on the tip of the tail, one on the right paw) and had written down how much we each weighed. She recorded our weight next to our "names" (right ear, left ear, tail tip, right paw). But whiteout fades, so once we got settled, Shelly set up a little nail salon on the floor.

She lined up four nail polish bottles: Flashy Fuchsia, Blue Me Away, Orange Zest, and High Line Green. She uses the same colors year after year and stores the bottles in a ziplock bag with the rest of her supplies. (If she has more kits, she uses one called Red Velvet Rope or another called Leapin' Lilac.)

Our claw color would match our bottle color.

RACCOON MANICURES

Shelly brushed a little paint on each of our claws and ta-da!

The Fab Four with our manicures. Miss Pink, Mr. Blue, Miss Orange in the back, and me, Mr. Green!

Miss Orange was a natural acrobat—a fuzzy little tumbler—from the very beginning, and also the squirmiest of our squad!

I, Mr. Green, have always been very clever. I was the first to figure out how to use the nipple on the bottle and, later, how to use a lot of our toys.

Mr. Blue was always at the top of our heap. He was the biggest and the strongest, and the ringleader of our little circus. From the first feeding, he was the fastest eater. It took Blue less than a minute to suck down his bottle!

Miss Pink was the smallest, and a real mama's girl. She was tiny, but before we could even walk and before our eyes even opened, she was always dragging her little body to be close to Shelly because she smelled the bottles!

49

As Shelly painted our claws, each of us made a huge dramatic fuss. We just hated being out of our warm mound and held up in the air that way. But it took only a few seconds. Shelly blew on our claws so the nail polish would dry faster; then she put us down. This wrestling match couldn't have been much fun for her either.

We stayed in our heap in the dark plastic carrier with layers of flannel cloth bedding underneath us. (She didn't use towels, as our tiny sharp claws could snag on them and twist our legs. She also had to make sure there were no holes in the flannel; we were so wiggly, we could have strangled ourselves. For such tiny things, we sure could get into a lot of trouble.) Shelly changed our bedding every few days and used special laundry detergent that didn't smell, as that could bother our lungs. In other words, we were fragile little critters!

Delicious formula came every three hours.

For the first few feedings, we drank from a syringe, like this one.

51

Soon we graduated to bottles, the same kind human babies use. Once a week, the bottles would be yucky, as they had a tiny bit of plain, unsweetened full-fat yogurt in them. We needed the yogurt's probiotics to keep our bellies healthy. We hated yogurt, but we still drank it.

Syringe feedings can be challenging.

The first feedings were like a three-way fussy-fight between us, the bottles, and Shelly's hand. Shelly had to clamp her hand around our muzzles to put our mouths on the nipple while she dripped formula into our mouths, but finally, we figured out what this new way of eating was all about. We were used to our mom's nipple, and the rubber bottle tip felt weird.

Miss Pink chewed the nipple instead of latching right on. Shelly had to massage her from her neck down to the base of her tail to "wake up" her suckling instinct. But Miss Pink figured it out the next day and started gulping her bottles like the rest of us.

Shelly started by measuring the formula powder in a big bottle, adding water, shaking it up, and keeping it in the refrigerator for at least four hours to let the powder dissolve.

Then she poured an exact amount of it into our bottles and heated them to exactly 100 degrees—not more, not less. She checked the temperature with a thermometer in a pan of hot water that held all four bottles at once. We needed to eat just enough at each feeding—not too much, not too little—in order to grow well, so she checked a chart in the WildCare guide, which she has posted on a cabinet near our containers of powdered formula (all foster caregivers use the same guide). Eventually we were all bottle pros, and we guzzled each bottle fast. We had lots of practice because we got six a day!

We all had to figure out how to make our mouths form a perfect seal around the nipples so air doesn't get in. If a kit is very small, weak, or sick, it can be tough for a human to get him or her into a smooth feeding routine.

Bottle-feeding is more complicated than it looks.

Shelly held us under our bellies, never on our backs. She let us push against the end of our bottles with our front paws. We also pawed at the air, as if we were pushing around our mom's nipples, to make the milk come out faster.

Shelly paid close attention to "nipple speed"—that's how fast the milk comes out of our bottles, and it depends on how large the hole is. When we're hungry, if we gulp too fast and take in too much formula and too many air bubbles, the formula bubbles out of our noses! When that happened, Shelly would stop, pull out the bottle, lower our heads to let the formula run out of our noses, and gently wipe it away.

That happened a lot with Mr. Blue because he was such a frantic eater. It's really quite dangerous, as formula can get into our lungs and cause pneumonia . . . or even kill us. Once, when Shelly held Mr. Blue to her ear, she heard a ragged "crackling" sound, which meant that there was fluid in his lungs. Six hours later, the sound was still there, so she took him back to WildCare for an exam, and then she had to give him liquid antibiotics from a syringe. We were scared when he left our pile, but he got better.

Sometimes, after we finished our bottles, we got the hiccups! Shelly also had to burp us because we couldn't burp on our own (just like human babies). If we didn't get burped, our stomachs could get upset. When we were finished drinking, Shelly used a damp washcloth to wipe our faces, necks, and chins. When formula dries, it's like glue. It can be very uncomfortable, and can even make our fur fall out. Our raccoon mom would have been licking us clean all over many times a day. Guess we're just a liiiittle bit high-maintenance!

Then, just like when we first got to the clinic, Shelly rubbed our bottoms to make us pee and poop. She cleaned us with wet wipes and put the dirty wipes in a Diaper Genie, just the way humans do for their babies.

But the whole process wasn't over. Our favorite part was still to come . . . suckle time!

Like human babies, we love to suckle. Sometimes we want that even more than a bottle. (If we were in the wild, we'd be with our moms almost all the time and we'd spend tons of time nursing on her, much longer than it takes us to finish a bottle.) So Shelly let each of us suck on a human infant's pacifier for almost fifteen minutes after we ate. A few years ago, one of her kits loved suckling so much that another volunteer sewed pacifiers onto the kit's bedding and onto a stuffed animal so she could suckle all the time!

Our suckling instinct is so strong that if

When we're full, our tummies look tight.

Shelly pulled the pacifier just a little bit into the air, we would clamp on, using the suction of our mouths, and would probably dangle from it if she lifted it! Sometimes we'll even suckle on one another's ears or other body parts. When we do that, Shelly has to look out for redness or swelling, and she might even have to separate us. (But we didn't do that.)

Only after *all* of this would we doze off, bellies round and full, and wait for the next bottle so it can start all over again. That's how we gain almost an ounce a day (the weight of a slice of bread) when we're very small!

Shelly's work didn't stop after teaching us to use the bottles. When we had medical problems, she treated us according to the WildCare vet's instructions. Her medicine cabinet was stocked with antibiotics, creams, and some medicine to deworm us. If we had eye infections, Shelly would hold hot, wet washcloths on our eyes. If we had diarrhea or gas, she gave us other medicines. She once cared for a kit who had a bone disease, and he needed sunlight every day for vitamin D. Shelly supervised him as he sat on the windowsill for thirty minutes every morning.

A few times, when we were really dirty, Shelly gave us baths in the bathroom sink! Rub-a-dub-dub, three kits in a tub.

It's hard to keep wild animals in a city apartment, but the humans had it all figured out. No one would ever think of us as pets. Our human team probably knew us almost as well as our real mom would have.

CHAPTER 5
EYES WiDE OPEN

We'd been at Shelly's for a week when our eyes slowly opened to our new world.

LOVELY LiTTLE LiLAC

One of the first things we saw, besides each other, was Shelly entering our room with a cardboard box much smaller than the one we'd arrived in.

Shelly set the box on the floor. Then she brought in an incubator. She set it carefully on top of a bookcase and plugged it in. Soon the inside of the

Lilac still had her umbilical cord.

incubator became hot—100 degrees and a little humid.

Shelly carefully lifted one lone kit, just one day old, out of the cardboard box. The kit was practically bald and as light as a feather—just over three ounces (85 grams), not even as heavy as a stick of butter. She was no bigger than a fuzzy kiwi, so we looked gigantic in comparison. The incubator was big enough for six kits her age, but the poor thing was all alone. Shelly put some stuffed animals around her (all raccoons!) so she wouldn't flop around.

The girl was even more helpless than we had been. Plus, we'd had one another. This kiwi just wriggled around with all four legs splayed out. But as Shelly set her down in the incubator, she told the little kit that she just might make it. "I got-choo," she whispered.

Shelly painted the kit's claws even though she was alone, as another kit her size could arrive at any time. She used the Leapin' Lilac nail polish for her manicure. We were quite a rainbow in there!

Shelly took Lilac out of the hot box every four hours to feed her with a syringe (even through the night!). Shelly was just like

A single kit is miserable alone. In nature we'd spend a whole year with our mom and siblings.

a mom with a newborn. Every time Lilac finished eating, she sucked on her tiny pacifier. But most of the time she just lay flat on her belly in her incubator under the warm light, all warm and floppy.

Lilac was teeny, but she had a big mouth! She yipped and purred, chittered and churred, and squealed and squeaked for Shelly.

She was the smallest baby Shelly had ever cared for, but she was a tough kit with lots of spirit. She kicked her little legs in the air, fighting and grunting quietly as Shelly held her in the palm of her hand.

Lilac could never join our cuddle club, as she was so much younger than we were. Later, though, she joined a litter her age and stayed with them until they were all big enough to go into the wild together.

Soon after our eyes opened, our ears opened too. Before that, they'd been flattened to our heads—now they popped right up! We heard Lilac going *eep, eep, eep* a lot, like a squeaky toy. She was crying for her mom, but she'd stop when Shelly picked her up to feed her.

We made more noises, and we heard one another "talking" all day and night.

HOW TO SPEAK RACCOON

All our noises mean something different.

chatter

eep

scream

trill

chirp

growl

screech

tweet

chitter

hiss

snarl

whimper

churr

mew

squeak

whinny

coo

purr

squeal

whistle

Miss Orange and Miss Pink became best buddies and playmates.

As we got bigger, we could play more—and be naughty. We still didn't roam free in the apartment; we'd never do that. And we never saw any other humans, even though Shelly's friends all wanted to meet us and play with us (of course!). We couldn't get too used to humans or other animals, for that would make us more likely to get into trouble with people or their pets once we were released. Even Shelly didn't play with us too much.

She encouraged us to play with one another, which we happily did.

When we turned four weeks old, Shelly opened the door to our carrier (which was set in the playpen). The playpen felt like our backyard! We also got to play on the floor when Shelly was there. Our world was getting bigger, and, of course, it would get much bigger still.

We were the Tumble Troop—rubbery little athletes! We were having so much fun.

Here's how all of us rescued raccoons live until we're released:

We move from the cat carrier to an open-top carrier.

When we're about
a month old, we're in
playpens (or a cat bed,
if Shelly can keep
an eye on us).

Then we move to the "Juvie Condo."

71

Soon we go to a small outdoor hutch.

Then we're in the large outdoor enclosure (at WildCare or on someone else's land).

Until recently we could only lift ourselves up on our front legs. But then we started to walk. For a few weeks, we looked really weird and wobbly, like little spiders! Mr. Blue was the strongest, and he moved well. If one of us was getting fed and the rest of us were waiting

Finally, when we're about five months old, off we go into the wild!

in the cat bed, Mr. Blue would crawl over the other two and smush them to get to Shelly next. We all hated waiting for the bottle!

We started grooming ourselves. We also started to pee and poop on our own, without

73

Shelly having to rub our bottoms. Now we peed and pooped everywhere!

Our rounded "bullet" noses had gotten pointier, and our face markings got clearer. And our baby teeth started to come in; Shelly could feel them budding through our gums. We were starting to look like real raccoons.

We looked like masked bandits!

CHAPTER 6

LIFE IN THE FUZZ PILE

We tumbled and turned somersaults. We wrestled and climbed and, as we always have, piled on top of one another. We loved to play rough, and when we fell, Shelly said it looked like we bounced!

"Who needs television when you can watch the kits?" Shelly said to a friend on the phone. "It's like having your own private circus . . . or the Raccoon Channel!"

Mr. Blue was the first to climb the playpen's netted walls (just as he would be the first to eventually climb a tree). Up, up, up Mr. Blue went, like Spider-Man, but when he reached the top, he just clung on for dear life. Our big, brave explorer didn't know what he'd gotten himself into! Shelly had to pry him off (tricky, with his sharp claws hanging on) and put him back in the pen. But soon enough he was climbing again . . . and so were we.

The playpen was the perfect place for us to play safely, but in every litter there's always one adventurous leader who tries to escape!

Because we were so ready to climb, we all got to practice on a climbing structure!

Mr. Blue soon figured out how to climb over the top of the playpen wall and down to the floor. This was possible because our hind legs can rotate—very convenient for climbing down trees.

CHECKING UP ON US

But we couldn't have constant climbing parties. Every two weeks, Shelly put us back in our carrier and drove us to WildCare for checkups. We got weighed, and sometimes we got vaccines, plus other medicine so that we wouldn't get worms. We'd been such tiny, blind kits the first time we were there, so we hadn't known what was happening around us. But now we saw just how busy the clinic really was. Vets, vet assistants, office staff, educators, and volunteers rushed around, taking care of hundreds of animals at once.

There was a whole room just for smaller birds—robins, pigeons, and the tiniest hummingbirds that needed to be fed with a dropper every twenty minutes! We always

entered through an area called the Wild Ambassador Courtyard, which had enclosures full of opossums, turtles, snakes, and more birds. Signs tell each animal's story and background information. These animals had come to WildCare injured, and the staff had tried and eventually been unable to get them ready to go back into the wild. They were called ambassadors, or teaching animals (they'd all shown that they could adjust to living around humans). They teach visitors about their species and their habitats and how to better share the world with wildlife.

Vladimir the turkey vulture was a famous ambassador. He'd been taken from his nest as a baby and kept at WildCare as a pet. He was thirty-two years old and had been there longer than any of the humans who worked there!

Once, we saw a WildCare teacher, Mary, with a third-grade class gathered around Vladimir. She was sharing facts about vultures, and a boy had his hand raised. "I wish Vlad didn't have to live in a cage," he said, his brow furrowed.

"I wish it too," Mary said. "I wish it so much. But if we're wishing that, and if we're sad and mad about it, then Vlad is doing his job. He's teaching people that wild animals belong in the wild. Then those people tell others about what they've learned here."

Another girl raised her hand. "I just don't want any of the ambassadors to be here at all," she said sternly.

Mary sighed. She'd heard this from lots of kids and adults. "I know it," she said. "And just like Vlad, the other ambassadors are doing their jobs too, so there will be fewer animals who have to come here at all."

When we entered the clinic, the first thing we saw were people cleaning, disinfecting, and sterilizing. They did this constantly because there are plenty of diseases and parasites they needed to avoid: parvovirus, distemper, ringworm, roundworm, and more. And the laundry room was in constant use, with stacks of towels and pillowcases that the humans used for everything from bedding for skunks to propping up injured birds so they could eat. In another room, cardboard crates and plastic carriers were stacked floor to ceiling.

At each visit, the staff saw that we were getting bigger and stronger for sure. "Nice work, Shelly," they'd say to her, smiling.

The raccoon team at WildCare has only one goal: big, healthy raccoons living free. When we're all grown up, our bodies look like mini sumo wrestlers . . . or large, chubby cats!

The oldest raccoon that humans know about was twenty-one years old, but there are so many dangers in the wild that we usually live only three to five years.

Our coats look like salt-and-pepper. Our thick, coarse undercoats keep water away from our skin, like a raincoat.

Our sensitive paw pads can feel texture especially well when they're wet.

We shuffle around on short legs. Our front legs are shorter than our hind legs.

Our tails have rings.

Our back feet rotate 180 degrees so we can turn and run headfirst down a tree. We're great climbers (but we can also survive a 35-foot fall)!

Our ears work so well that we can hear an earthworm burrowing, and we can hear other raccoons making sounds from far away to warn of danger.

Our "masks" may reduce glare to help us see better at night.

Our eyes look like shiny black marbles. Like cats, we have a special layer of tissue in our eyes that helps our night vision.

We can smell the scent trail of other raccoons. We keep "smell maps" in our head so that we can stay connected to our dens, food sources, and one another.

We have long, furry, delicate fingers with flexible thumbs. Like humans', our hands can grab and grasp.

Even as babies, our tiny claws are needle-sharp!

Our bodies are perfect for just hanging out!

PART 3

REHABILITATION

Playing and Preparing

CHAPTER 7

CHALLENGES, PLEASE

We were in for another adventure. Our first hint was this: once we finished our bottles and cried for more, Shelly would put tiny tastes of persimmon syrup or applesauce on her gloved fingertip and let us lick it off. It was the first taste we had of anything but formula, and it was the beginning of weaning—fewer bottles and more "real food." We were seven weeks old, now called "juvies" (short for juvenile, or young). Just as we had figured out how to drink from our bottles, we gradually learned to eat lots of different kinds of food.

Our first solid food was raccoon custard,

Weaning custard was a scrumptious mess.

made from eggs, powdered formula and nutrients, and persimmons. We loved crunchy eggshells!

Marie-Noelle developed this recipe for weaning mush, and we loved that, too.

RECIPE

Mushy Crunchy Salad

- cut-up grapes
- soaked kibble
- warm persimmons—previously frozen as to be extra-sweet and syrupy

Mush ingredients together and top with custard-stuffed eggshells for added texture and calcium!

Soon enough we had a long menu. With raccoons, the more variety, the better.

We ate fruit, protein, and carbohydrates
from heavy bowls that we couldn't flip over.

Shelly's Weaning Café

Fruit

- Grapes helped us learn to chew food.
- Soon we got more fruit (we're sugar freaks, and we prefer fruit over veggies!): avocado, watermelon, persimmon, mango, sweet plum, banana, and applesauce.
- Later, we got apples, peaches, plums, pears, and cherries (never citrus).

Protein

- After weaning custard, we got eggs: scrambled, soft-boiled, and raw.
- Then we got small dead animals from Shelly's freezer: baby chicks, smelts (fish), and mice. She thawed them in the fridge and even chopped them up!
- We also got nuts—almonds were our favorite.

Carbs

- We ate dry puppy food soaked in water and microwaved into mush!
- Then we got corn (on the cob and off!), acorns, and sweet potatoes.

Live Foods

- Soon after that, we got clams and oysters. We learned to pry them apart with our paws!
- Once we had a kiddie pool outdoors, we got goldfish, crayfish, and crabs (which we ripped the claws off of). In the wild, though, we'd prefer acorns, corn, seeds, shoots, and buds.

Treats

Shelly had to keep us from having too much sugar. Once in a while we got a Fig Newton, but we were also happy with berries, cheese bits, and dog biscuits.

GRAPES ARE GREAT
By me, Mr. Green

One day, Shelly gently pushed a small green grape into my mouth and pressed my jaw together until I felt a squish. But the sweet juice just dripped to the floor. It took only one more grape for me to catch on—if I threw my head back, I'd be able to swallow all the juice! Shelly loved watching us learn new things.

AVOCADOS AND THEIR PITS
By Miss Orange

Of all the fruit, avocados were my favorite. Shelly would cut one in half, leaving in the pit. I learned fast to put my paws on it, hold it down, and nibble away until my face was green.

Having Shelly as a waitress was great, but it was also important for us to learn how to find food in the wild. So Shelly made us work for it. It looked as if we were playing, but we were practicing a survival skill. Shelly created games for our School for Foragers:

- **A Dozen Grapes:** Shelly put a grape in each compartment of an egg carton and closed the carton.

- **Scavenger Hunt:** She hid treats, and we had to find them.

- **Get It Out!:** She put treats in bags and plastic containers that had holes in the lid so we could practice reaching and scooping. (Because we eat leftovers from garbage cans, we need to be able to open sealed containers and bags—anything we might find in the trash. Some humans say *Ewww* when they hear what we eat, but I think they should say *Oooh* instead—*Oooh*, look how fast we learned to survive when humans started taking away our habitat. We don't let much go to waste!).

As we got even more active, we needed more space to play and exercise, and Shelly had just the spot! We were finally old enough to move into the Juvie Condo.

CHAPTER 8

PERFECT PLAYGROUNDS

The Juvie Condo was really a ferret cage, but it was perfect for us. It was three stories tall—taller than Shelly—with little staircases connecting the floors. When guests came to visit, Shelly covered it with a sheet.

The Juvie Condo was like a playground and an apartment all in one!

We had tons of toys in our condo. Often, Shelly would take some away and add new ones to keep us challenged. Many of them were from nature, such as acorns, pinecones, pieces of branch, bark, limestone chunks, stones, pebbles, shells, maple keys, and flower-seed heads.

Our great sense of touch made texture and feel really important, and Shelly found interesting things for us, such as crinkly cellophane, sheets of aluminum foil, or boxes made of corrugated cardboard for us to open and scratch.

Bubble wrap was one of our favorite textures.

OUR TERRIFIC TOYBOX

Play is our work. It's how we learn what we need to know in order to survive. We got human baby toys—plastic key rings and rattles—and toddler toys—stacking rings and a wire roller coaster with blocks (we love to bang those blocks around!). We got dog toys, such as chew toys and squeaky balls, and cat toys, such as balls with bells inside and "crinkly" balls. We also got rabbit toys—wicker balls and a tunnel made of straw!

We learn a lot by watching one another play,
and we love challenges. Once we solve a
problem, we're ready for another!

We drank plenty of fresh, clean water from a heavy bowl. We played with the water, too, which would become important later. Our paw pads are most sensitive when they're wet, and that helps us to be better hunters. Our paws are pretty sensitive in the first place. They have thousands of nerve endings that let us "see the world with our feet." We can rub garbage between our paws to figure out what part of it is edible (for instance, if there is a little piece of a burrito wrapped in foil, we can find and eat the burrito—not the foil!).

That's why we dip our paws in streams and rivers, to get them as sensitive as we can. We look like we're washing, but we're really dabbling for underwater food. Then we pick the food up with both front paws. We rub it and check it out with our paws. That's how we clean it and remove the parts we don't want.

tree! Up we went. Our claws came in so handy! Climbing up was ridiculously easy.

Getting down, not so easy. We all trilled for help (the sound we would have made for our mom), but Mr. Blue figured out how to climb down, and we watched carefully. He turned himself around with his rotating back legs the way he had when he climbed down from the playpen, and we all followed. It worked, and then we were back on the ground, leaves crunching under our paws.

We didn't need Shelly to bring us food in metal bowls here, of course. Instead we foraged like real raccoons! There was a banquet in front of us—raspberries on bushes and live grubs under fallen logs. We found insects on the ground and grabbed them with our paws, rolling them around on our paw pads and then gobbling them up. Shelly showed us

FiELD TRIPS

A day to remember!

a freshwater stream we could wade in, and that's when the fun really started. We knew just what to do—we rubbed water on our front feet and felt around for fish and snails.

We wanted to stay much longer than Shelly had planned. Finally, she had to scoop each of us up and put us back in the carrier ... all except Mr. Blue, who was exploring a treetop and saw no reason to stop. But like all littermates, we hated being alone and apart from one another, so when Shelly started walking away with our carriers, he began to call out for us. We called right back, and when he heard us, he rushed down and jumped right into the carrier so we wouldn't leave without him!

We were still a terrific team.

CHAPTER 9

WILDING UP

Field trips were just sneak previews of what was coming next. At ten weeks, we got moved to an outdoor hutch at a volunteer's home (there's another hutch at WildCare, but some volunteers build them on their own property). One volunteer, Rachel, had built a small hutch off the ground. It was a

We still got one or two bottles a day in the hutch, but we were almost completely weaned.

step above the Juvie Condo, and living there meant that we could now breathe fresh air 24/7!

Brunch in the hutch!

Things got even better a couple of weeks later when we moved to Rachel's large outdoor enclosure right on the ground, which felt like our own private playground. Once we get to these types of enclosures, we barely see humans. They put food down when we're asleep and clean up only when they really have to. This was as close as we could get to the wild for another nine weeks. Humans design and build these enclosures

very carefully, thinking only of what we need:

- a roof to help us feel hidden and safe

- high nest boxes filled with dried grass, with ramps for going in and out

- ropes for hanging and swinging

- hammocks made of tough fabric and thick rope

- a ladder for climbing practice

- branches

- a tire swing

- a big hardwood stump

- hollow logs

- carpet tubes to use as tunnels

- a Wiffle Ball on a rope between two nest boxes (so we can pull the ball back and forth)

- a kiddie pool for water play

- Ping-Pong balls (we chase them to practice hunting!)

- a hollow tree stump

- a milk crate hanging from a bungee (great for swinging!)

- plenty of our "school supplies": pinecones, rocks, acorns, bark, moss, and more

LIFE IN THE HUTCH

HOUSEWARMING GIFTS

As if life in the big enclosure wasn't great enough, Shelly and other volunteers brought us surprises. Their goals were to fatten us up and keep us from getting bored. They brought:

- a watermelon

- an old Christmas tree with pinecones and shrimp hanging from the branches

- colored balls that floated in the kiddie pool

- presents to unwrap (with treats inside)

- a rotting log with mealworms (that didn't last long!)

- a "special challenge" wooden box with locks all over it (A volunteer who was a woodworker made it just for raccoons, and we figured out how to unlock all the locks in twenty minutes.)

Rachel peeked in on us plenty and brought us more treats, such as live crickets, crabs, goldfish, and shrimp (all of which they put in the kiddie pool). The people watched us carefully to see if we were finding hidden food, climbing in the more challenging places, and staying healthy. We all were! We got all we wanted to eat, twice a day. The humans were focused on our weight gain so we could get through our first winter. (In colder climates, when there's not as much food, raccoons can lose half their weight over a winter.) In any case, a fat raccoon is a safer raccoon.

Crabs are a raccoon favorite!

RELEASE

Becoming Free

RACCOON ROAD

After a magical two months in the large enclosure, it was finally time for the human team to plan for our release. According to their list of strict requirements, we were ready!

For a safe release, raccoons must:

- be in good health (and parasite-free) and up to date on vaccinations
- be at least sixteen weeks (four months) old
- weigh at least eight pounds (3.6 kilograms) (with a good layer of fat)
- have lived with at least two other raccoons outdoors for at least two weeks
- recognize natural food and be able to compete with their littermates for food
- have healthy permanent canine teeth
- have stayed healthy on their own for at least two weeks
- not want anything to do with humans!

The night before a release, the humans fed us even more than usual.

It was important for them to choose exactly the right place to release us. There had to be a permanent water source—a lake, marsh, river, stream, or pond—and lots of trees. They used a computer program that showed the land from above.

If the humans had a choice, our new home would be at least two miles away from roads, buildings, or houses. An oak woodland habitat would be perfect because there are so many acorns. Oak trees produce tons of them, and they feed lots of different animals; and Marin County, has tons of red, white, black, and golden oaks. Ideally our new habitat shouldn't be home to too many other raccoons (especially ones that grew up in the wild). That way we're not all fighting over food.

No matter where we wound up, our main job would be to fit in with any raccoons living there and find a good den site before November, when it would start getting cold and wet.

DEN CHOICES

Female raccoons need the dark, safe
shelter of a den (males can sleep in
tree branches). Raccoons don't always
have a choice of where it is, but a den
can be:

 a hole in or under a log

 the inside of a hollow
tree

 a nook in a rocky
ledge or cave

 the empty burrow
of another animal,
like a woodchuck,
in the ground or on a
riverbank

 a space under a log or rock

 in a barn, garage, rain sewer, shed,
basement, or attic, or under a house

We get close to humans' homes only when
we're hungry or desperate (for example, if a
female needs a den to protect her babies).

We were lucky to be released at the end
of September, at nearly five months old.
If we're born too late in the spring, or if
we're not big enough for release by twenty
weeks, we're stuck in the enclosure until
the following spring. We would have to have
well-insulated nest boxes to protect us from
the colder, wetter weather. (In colder places,
we wouldn't get released till we were at least
six months old.)

If we're going to live near where the outdoor
enclosure is, we will get "soft released,"
which means that the humans just open the
door of the enclosure and let us come and
go. They leave "support feedings" and water
until we go off to den, when the humans are
sure we've found a food and water source
for ourselves. Some of us will disappear
for days or even a week to explore our new
world. Others are wilder and never show up

again. Either way, the humans keep leaving the food out. It's similar to training wheels or a safety net.

In any case, our group got a "hard release" because our enclosure was too close to automobile traffic—we went straight from enclosure to nature, no in-between. The humans kept checking the forecast and waiting for a three-day stretch of dry, warm weather.

Shelly, Rachel, and Amanda (another WildCare volunteer) planned every detail. Rachel had a friend who owned lots of land not far away from where we were born, and the friend said she'd be happy to have us live on her property.

So late one afternoon when we were snoozing in our nest boxes, the humans came

Once again, the humans were in charge.
But this time it wouldn't be for long, because this
was no field trip. And we kind of knew it.

for us, trying to push us into two carriers. It was funny—when we were little, we really loved those hands, but now they were covered in leather gloves. Shelly and Rachel were calm but determined. We ran away and squirmed and screeched—why were they trying to catch and trap us? They'd been so cool about leaving us alone in the enclosure. Shelly and Rachel had to scruff us, one by one, and pick us up off the ground (we hated that—we know that nothing good ever happens when our feet aren't on something solid).

We put up a good fight, but when the humans finally won, they pushed us (carefully enough, of course) into the carriers—two of us in each. They covered the carriers in towels.

They put our carriers in the small back seat

This would be our new home.

of a four-wheel-drive truck. We screeched
the whole time, clawing constantly at the
gates, tops, and sides of the crates. We
hated being apart, and we poked our paws
through the bars, trying to touch our siblings

in the other carrier. The trip seemed to last forever. As the truck slowed down, it was almost dusk.

The late-afternoon sun was lighting up the fog. The whole world seemed to be lit up in misty pink and gold. It was all happening.

CHAPTER 11

THE FOREST, FINALLY

Good thing the truck had four-wheel drive, because the dirt road leading to our new home was narrow, zigzaggy, and rocky. We were so far out that the humans' cell phones stopped working. They'd chosen a spot on the side of a mountain, on five hundred acres owned by the same family for more than a hundred years! "There's plenty of land to share," the landowner said, laughing.

Shelly, Rachel, and Amanda hauled our carriers to a pond and positioned us so that the carrier doors faced the pond. Then Rachel quietly opened our doors, and Shelly started taking photos.

After all our fuss about getting into the carriers, now we were freaked out by the idea of leaving them.

But there wasn't much to photograph, because we were frozen in place.

Of course, Mr. Blue started moving his head around and sniffing the air first. He poked his nose out beyond the door, then quickly pulled himself back in. Then he poked out again, continuing this routine until all but his tail was outside the carrier.

Here are five different litters being released at different times, but we all do the same thing— we come out slowly and grow more and more curious!

As usual, the rest of us watched carefully.
Just as he did on the field trip, he climbed
right onto the top of the carrier. But this was
no field trip. This time we wouldn't be going
back with Shelly.

Next went Miss Orange, then Miss Pink.
They circled both carriers, sniffing them,
putting their front paws on one to get a
better look at what Mr. Blue was doing up
top. I stayed in my carrier for a while longer,
but soon all of us were playing around and
on top of the carriers and scampering back
in and out of them.

At one point, I had the roof of one carrier
to myself, but I shifted my weight and the
carrier toppled right over me and rolled
down a little hill! The humans cracked up,
and we all had to check it out and play inside
that crate ... one more time.

The moon hadn't risen yet. It was quiet.

It was just warm enough, about 65 degrees.
It was still light, and the air was cool and crisp.
It was fall, so everything had become
dry and dusty.

Mr. Blue seemed seriously ready to disappear
into the woods. He made a bold move and
walked right past the humans into some
thick brush near the pond. Soon the rest of us

135

The whole place was exploding with the newness that we love so much. It was half overwhelming and half thrilling.

were brave enough to slip into the tall reeds surrounding the mosquito-filled water (Shelly already had eleven bug bites on her legs and arms!). There were so many high, dry, sharp "poky" reeds around the pond that the people couldn't get up to its edge. But we could!

I was the last one to disappear into the wild, just after I heard Rachel whisper, "Excellent. We don't want them running toward us."

The pond was surrounded by tall trees. We knew it was time to climb one, and we made it look easy! Once we got up a bit, Miss Pink and Miss Orange stayed side by side, clinging to the same branch while I found one of my own. Mr. Blue remained with all four legs wrapped on the thick trunk. King of the tree!

"This is good," Shelly said. "The higher they go up in that tree, the better."

The humans watched us for a while, then picked up the empty carriers and started walking away. Soon we couldn't see them at all. They were leaving our woodsy world. "Go have a great time, guys!" Shelly called up to us. "You know what to do!" Then she turned to the others, smiling big. "I hope we never see them again," she said.

About one second later, we turned all our attention to dinner. Our days would now be all about exploring and foraging. And so the forest feasting began.

CHAPTER 12
THE BiG, WIDE WOODS

While Mr. Blue and I were still high up in the tree, Miss Orange and Miss Pink explored the edge of the pond. They wet their paws and began with an appetizer of yellow jackets and grubs. They rolled them around between their palms. Yup, good to eat. Then Miss Orange moved fast . . . and caught her first small frog!

Mr. Blue expertly climbed down from the tree and became obsessed with acorns on the ground, and when I finally scampered down, he found an egg that had fallen from a nest and happily held it delicately in both hands, nibbling away.

Here we finally are, right where we are meant to be.

Our first dinner in the wild was easy and delicious, but we'd be constantly learning new things. We'd been pooping in a "shared latrine" since we moved to the enclosure, but we'd never smelled other raccoons' poop before. It turned out that all raccoons in the area share the same "poop patch." It helps us know who else is around.

We wish our mom could see us now.

We also didn't know that young raccoons are the "bosses" out here, so, luckily, we wouldn't have to worry about any trouble with other raccoons. There's a very nice reason for this. Our moms would have still been really protective of us out here, so when another adult sees a young raccoon, they assume its mom is nearby and ready to defend it.

As sisters, Miss Pink and Miss Orange will find dens and stick pretty close together until spring (at least half of our cuddle pile will still exist!). They won't look for their own dens until they get pregnant. By December, we'll all go off on our own a little more, but we'll stay in the same territory and see one another.

Maybe we'll see Lilac and her adopted littermates here one day. We hope so. She

was doing great the last time we saw her,
but that feels like such a long time ago.

We'll face some challenges for sure, as much
as all wild animals do. Out here, there are
droughts, heatwaves, and wildfires, plus
predators. But that's life in the woods. And
no matter what, we'll stay clever and curious.
We'll keep our paws wet. We'll hunt and we'll
climb and we'll rest safe in our dens.

The redwood trees are so tall, it feels like
a dream. There's a waterfall that splashes
into a creek filled with crayfish. The acorns
pile up like pebbles on a beach. And then, of
course, there's us . . .

The Fab Four.

A LETTER FROM THE AUTHOR: RACCOONS RULE!

I met Shelly Ross and Marie-Noelle Marquis on a visit to WildCare. Shelly had brought her litter in for a checkup and was catching up with Marie-Noelle, the head of the raccoon team. We talked about their work and the book I hoped to write. I wasn't yet sure whether my book should be about raccoons, opossums, squirrels, skunks, or another animal that came through WildCare's doors. As I was asking what must have seemed like the hundredth question, Shelly told Marie-Noelle that it was time to feed the four kits. Then they said I could observe the feeding from a distance.

We went into a dark, quiet office. Shelly gently lifted a tiny kit from the carrier, and I watched the whole routine (bottle, burp, suckle, pee, poop, and clean). They fed them one by one, and I couldn't take my eyes from the scene. I knew then that I wanted to write a book about raccoons. There were two main reasons.

First, lots of people don't like these creatures, but most people don't understand their situation and don't realize how clever and adaptable they are.

Second, raccoons are everything I'd like to be. They see problems as opportunities to learn something new. They use their natural curiosity and cleverness to survive and thrive in bad situations. They "bounce back." They get used to change quickly. They're brave explorers and fast, flexible thinkers.

They learn by watching one another, and I learned a lot by watching them. I hope everyone who reads this book will feel as if they've gotten a good peek into the lives of raccoons, too!

— Kama Ainhun

Crawling courageously forward!

THREE QUICK QUESTIONS FOR SHELLY ROSS

Q: How did you get started as a wildlife rehabilitator?

A: *On a trip to Africa, I volunteered at a lion refuge. When I got home, I knew I wanted to keep working with wildlife. At the time, I didn't even know that wildlife rehabilitation was a thing! I Googled "volunteering with wildlife," and WildCare popped up. Their volunteer orientation was in less than a month. I signed up, and I've been doing this ever since!*

Q: What's it like to live alone and then suddenly have four new raccoon roommates?

A: *You really have to be willing to put your life on hold for baby season. I'm lucky to have a schedule that lets me be so involved. It's incredibly time-consuming and a lot of work, but I love every minute of it. Watching them develop is such a privilege. It's completely worth it.*

Q: Is one particular raccoon age your favorite?

A: *No. There's something magical and wondrous about each one. They start out so completely dependent on humans, and they end up not wanting anything to do with us, which I take as a compliment on a job well done.*

HOW YOU CAN HELP

There are so many ways you can help raccoons and other woodland animals such as skunks, opossums, birds, squirrels, and more. You can count them on a raccoon's paws—five claws on each paw equals twenty claws.

1 BE A GOOD NEIGHBOR

If you see a sick or hurt wild animal, tell a grownup before going any closer. Together, call a wildlife expert for advice. (Some animals are just waiting for their moms to come back with food, and birds might be taking a little rest when they're learning to fly.) The apps Animal Help Now (ahnow. org) and WildHelp (wildhelp.org) show you your closest wildlife rescue and rehabilitation groups. So does this website: *http://wildliferehabber. com/wildlife-agency-listing.*

- Remind grownups to slow down when driving in order to avoid hitting animals that are crossing the road.

- Don't feed raccoons or wild animals. Raccoons that are fed by people can lose their fear of humans and may become aggressive when not

Watch for raccoons crossing roads.

fed the way they've learned to expect. Also, our food can make other wild animals sick.

- Rinse containers before you recycle them so animals don't get their heads stuck inside when trying to lick food from them. Cut apart six-pack soda tops before throwing them away—sea birds and other marine life can get caught in them or eat them. Avoid using balloons (many animals mistake them for food).

- If you're eating in the car, avoid throwing leftovers out the window. Animals go into the road or at the roadside to eat food that's been thrown from car windows, and they can be hit by cars.

2 HELP PETS AND WILDLIFE LIVE TOGETHER

- Feed dogs and cats inside. If they must eat outside, feed them in late morning or at midday, and pick up food, water bowls, leftovers, and spilled food well before dark every day.

- Keep pets inside at night. Wildlife and pets may injure or kill one another.

- Prevent raccoons from entering pet doors.

- Keep food away from pet doors and lock them at night. If you have to keep them open, put an electronically activated opener on your pet's collar.

- More than two billion birds are killed by domestic cats every year. Keep cats inside, or consider building a catio (a screened-in porch).

3 KEEP RACCOONS AWAY

- If wildlife is causing trouble in or around your home, talk with your family about figuring out

151

Humans can raccoon-proof their houses
so that this doesn't happen.

what's attracting them and remove it or put out safe, poison-free deterrents (instead of trapping them or calling an exterminator). Search for "wildlife exclusion" in your area. (In Northern California, call WildCare Solutions at 415-453-1000 x23.)

- "Raccoon-proof" your house or garage. Raccoons (and mice, rats, and other mammals) use chimneys, attics, and spaces under houses, porches, and sheds as den sites. Find out how to close up possible entrances (and make sure you don't trap an animal inside).

- Put garbage in cans and make sure the lids are on tight. Secure lids with rope, chain, bungee cords, or weights. Ask grownups to buy garbage cans with clamps that hold lids on. To prevent tipping, secure side handles to metal or wooden stakes driven into the ground, or keep cans in tight-fitting bins, a shed, or a garage.

- Put garbage cans out for pickup in the morning, after raccoons have returned to their resting areas.

- Don't attract raccoons! Make sure outdoor grills are clean, and if you have a compost area, make sure it's raccoon-proof.

4 TEACH, LEARN, AND DONATE

- If you're in Northern California, visit WildCare in San Rafael (discoverwildcare.org).

- You may not live near an urban wildlife sanctuary such as WildCare, but there are animal shelters and sanctuaries almost everywhere. Learn about the animals that share your habitat, and meet the people who help them. You can learn a lot about animals without visiting a zoo!

- When you have a choice of topics for a school project, choose an animal that's facing challenges in your area.

- Share what you've learned. Tell your family and friends what you know about being a good neighbor to wildlife. Remind people that wild animals aren't pets.

- Instead of presents for your birthday, ask for donations to your local wildlife clinic. Or have a bake sale or lemonade stand to raise money for them. (You can find the clinics by using the apps listed above.)

BiBLiOGRAPHY

Raccoon Nation. PBS *Nature*, 2012.

Don Juan, Deutsche . *Raccoon: Beautiful Pictures & Interesting Facts.* CreateSpace, 2015.

easyscienceforkids.com/all-about-raccoons/.

Johnson, J. Angelique, *Raccoons (Nocturnal Animals).* North Mankato, MN: Capstone Press, 2011.

kids.nationalgeographic.com/animals/raccoon/.

Read, Tracey C. *Exploring the World of Raccoons.* Richmond Hill, Ontario: Firefly Books, 2010.

www.wildliferescueleague.org/for_kids.

PHOTO CREDITS

All photographs by Shelly Ross except:

dedication page: Noel Brinkerhoff

8, 79: Alison Hermance

26, 38: Marie-Noelle Marquis

30, 31: Courtesy of WildCare

45: Kama Einhorn

123: Corbis

128: Getty Images (Florian Kainz)

GLOSSARY

adapt: adjust or get used to

carbohydrate: sugars (such as fruit) and starches (such as potatoes or bread) that give mammals' bodies energy

ecosystem: a community of animals and plants living together in an area; a system in which living things interact with the weather, the sun, air, water, and soil around them

environment: the surroundings in which people or animals live

forage: search for food

foster: raise a person or animal that is not yours by birth

habitat: the natural home of an animal

hydrated: having enough water in one's body

instinct: a natural way of thinking or acting, a fixed pattern of doing something

juvenile: not fully grown

nocturnal: sleeping during the day and being active at night

omnivore: an animal that eats all kinds of food

predator: an animal that eats other animals

protect: keep from harm

pry: open something that's hard to open, such as a clamshell

recover: get better

rehabilitate: return to one's natural condition

release: let go, set free

rescue: save or help

sanctuary: a safe place

scavenger: an animal that eats garbage or dead or rotted animals or plants

stable: a condition in which a living thing's health is not getting any worse

surrogate: a substitute

survive: continue to live even in the face of danger or challenges

wean: get a young mammal used to food other than milk or formula

ACKNOWLEDGMENTS

Special thanks to:

Erica Blue, Alison Hermance,

Cassius Kloehn, Gregory Kloehn,

Silas Kloehn, Marie-Noelle

Marquis, Vaughn Maurice,

Melanie Piazza, Mary Pounder, Shelly Ross, Juliana Sorem,

DVM, the Entire Team at WildCare, and to JoLynn Taylor, whose

guide, *Foster Care Manual 2.0: Raccoons: Captive Rearing

Protocol*, was invaluable in the writing of this book

INDEX

TRUE TALES of RESCUE

Available now!

Coming soon!

Kama Einhorn is a humane educator, animal welfare advocate, and author of more than forty books for children and teachers. Animals are her people. She lives in Brooklyn, New York.